# WEDDING MUSIC
## FOR CLASSICAL PLAYERS

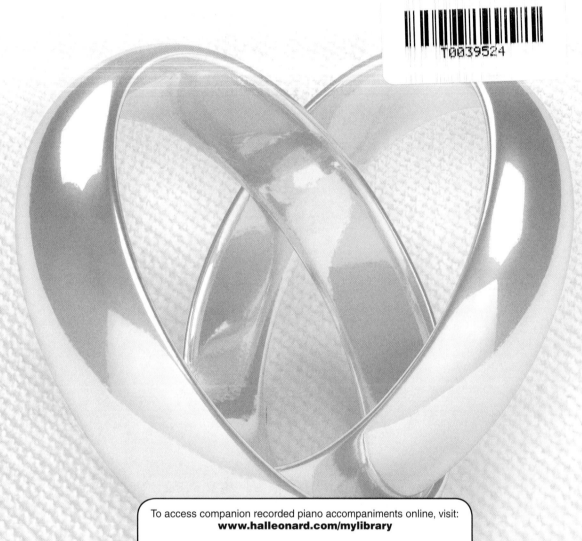

To access companion recorded piano accompaniments online, visit:
**www.halleonard.com/mylibrary**

Enter Code
2974-2934-2629-3037

ISBN: 978-1-5400-2044-4

Visit Hal Leonard Online at
**www.halleonard.com**

Contact Us:
**Hal Leonard**
7777 West Bluemound Road
Milwaukee, WI 53213
Email: info@halleonard.com

In Europe contact:
**Hal Leonard Europe Limited**
42 Wigmore Street
Marylebone, London, W1U 2RN
Email: info@halleonardeurope.com

In Australia contact:
**Hal Leonard Australia Pty. Ltd.**
4 Lentara Court
Cheltenham, Victoria, 3192 Australia
Email: info@halleonard.com.au

Depending on the situation, sometimes wedding service music must be abbreviated or expanded. Feel free to find optional cuts, endings, or repeated sections as needed.

# CONTENTS

Pianists on the recordings: [1]Brendan Fox, [2]Richard Walters

The price of this publication includes access to companion recorded piano accompaniments online,

for download or streaming, using the unique code found on the title page.

Visit www.halleonard.com/mylibrary and enter the access code.

# Air
## from Orchestral Suite No. 3 in D Major, BWV 1068

Johann Sebastian Bach
Transcribed by Celeste Avery

# Arioso
## (Sinfonia)
### from Cantata, BWV 156

Johann Sebastian Bach
Transcribed by Celeste Avery

# The Prince of Denmark's March

Jeremiah Clarke
Transcribed by Celeste Avery

# Ave Maria
adapted from Prelude in C Major, BWV 846 by Johann Sebastian Bach

Charles Gounod
Transcribed by Celeste Avery

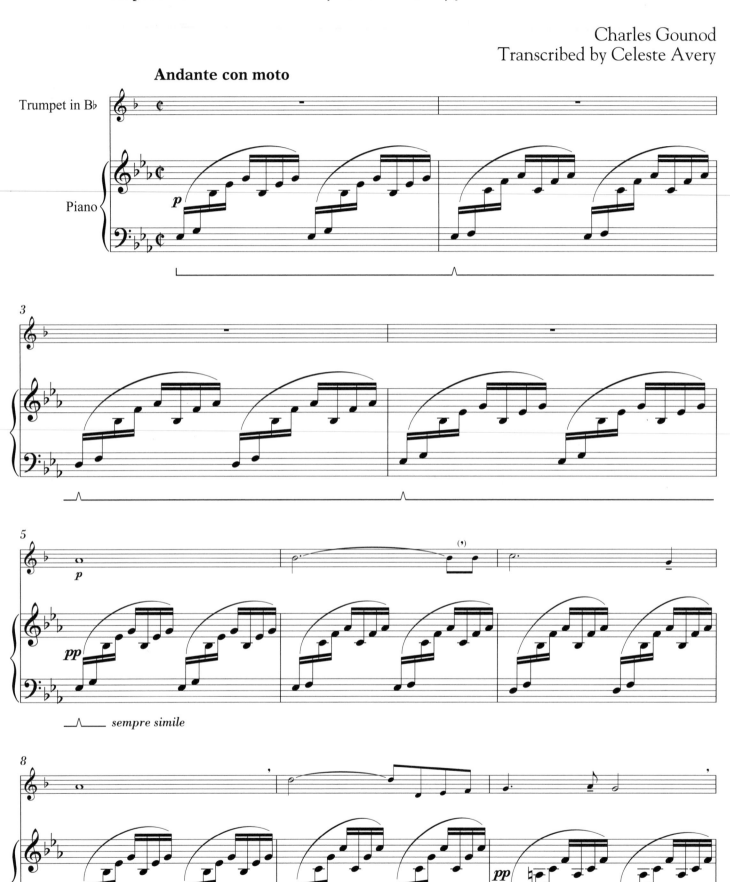

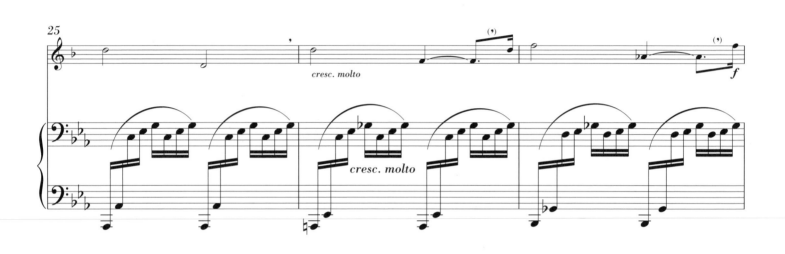

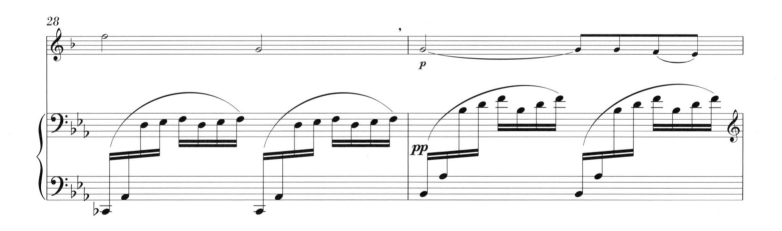

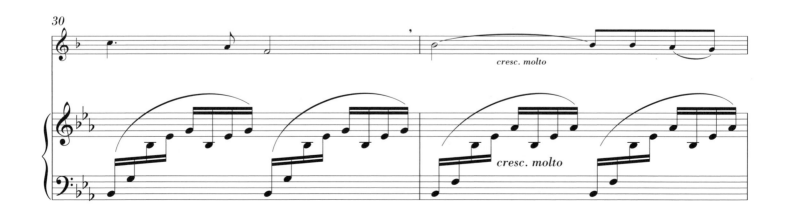

# Hornpipe
from *Water Music*, HWV 348

George Frideric Handel
Transcribed by Celeste Avery

# Largo
### (Ombra mai fù)
### from *Serse*, HWV 40

George Frideric Handel
Transcribed by Celeste Avery

# Jupiter Chorale
## from *The Planets*

Gustav Holst
Transcribed by Celeste Avery

# Wedding March

from *A Midsummer Night's Dream*, Op. 61

Felix Mendelssohn
Transcribed by Celeste Avery

# Rondeau
from *Suite of Symphonies* No. 1

Jean-Joseph Mouret
Transcribed by Celeste Avery

# WEDDING MUSIC
## FOR CLASSICAL PLAYERS

To access companion recorded piano accompaniments online, visit:
**www.halleonard.com/mylibrary**

Enter Code
5651-2158-3841-7380

ISBN: 978-1-5400-2044-4

## HAL•LEONARD®

Visit Hal Leonard Online at
**www.halleonard.com**

Contact Us:
**Hal Leonard**
7777 West Bluemound Road
Milwaukee, WI 53213
Email: info@halleonard.com

In Europe contact:
**Hal Leonard Europe Limited**
42 Wigmore Street
Marylebone, London, W1U 2RN
Email: info@halleonardeurope.com

In Australia contact:
**Hal Leonard Australia Pty. Ltd.**
4 Lentara Court
Cheltenham, Victoria, 3192 Australia
Email: info@halleonard.com.au

Depending on the situation, sometimes wedding service music must be abbreviated or expanded.
Feel free to find optional cuts, endings, or repeated sections as needed.

# CONTENTS

Pianists on the recordings: [1]Brendan Fox, [2]Richard Walters

The price of this publication includes access to companion recorded piano accompaniments online,

for download or streaming, using the unique code found on the title page.

Visit **www.halleonard.com/mylibrary** and enter the access code.

# Air
from Orchestral Suite No. 3 in D Major, BWV 1068

Johann Sebastian Bach
Transcribed by Celeste Avery

\* This repeat is omitted on the companion accompaniment recording.

The pianist plays the following as an introduction on the companion accompaniment recording:

# Arioso
## (Sinfonia)
from Cantata, BWV 156

Johann Sebastian Bach
Transcribed by Celeste Avery

The pianist plays the following as an introduction on the companion accompaniment recording:

# The Prince of Denmark's March

Jeremiah Clarke
Transcribed by Celeste Avery

The pianist plays measure 24 as an introduction on the companion accompaniment recording.

# Ave Maria

adapted from Prelude in C Major, BWV 846 by Johann Sebastian Bach

Charles Gounod
Transcribed by Celeste Avery

# Hornpipe
from *Water Music, HWV 348*

George Frideric Handel
Transcribed by Celeste Avery

**Allegro**

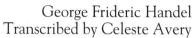

# Largo
(Ombra mai fù)

from *Serse*, HWV 40

George Frideric Handel
Transcribed by Celeste Avery

**Larghetto**

# Jupiter Chorale

from *The Planets*

Gustav Holst
Transcribed by Celeste Avery

The pianist plays the following as an introduction on the companion accompaniment recording:

# Wedding March

from *A Midsummer Night's Dream*, Op. 61

Felix Mendelssohn
Transcribed by Celeste Avery

# Rondeau

from *Suite of Symphonies* No. 1

Jean-Joseph Mouret
Transcribed by Celeste Avery

The pianist plays the following as an introduction on the companion accompaniment recording:

# Canon
(Canon in D)

Johann Pachelbel
Transcribed by Celeste Avery

# Trumpet Tune

Henry Purcell
Transcribed by Christopher Ruck

**Stately**

The pianist plays measures 23–24 as an introduction on the companion accompaniment recording.

# Gymnopédie No. 1

from *Trois Gymnopédies*

Erik Satie
Transcribed by Celeste Avery

For a shorter performance, the piece may begin at measure 40.

# Ave Maria

Franz Schubert
Transcribed by Celeste Avery

# Bist du bei mir
## (You Are with Me)

Gottfried Heinrich Stölzel
Transcribed by Celeste Avery

# Bridal Chorus

from *Lohengrin*

Richard Wagner
Transcribed by Celeste Avery

* For a shorter version, begin here after four measures of introduction.

# Bridal Chorus
## from *Lohengrin*

Richard Wagner
Transcribed by Celeste Avery

* For a shorter version, begin here after four measures of introduction.

# Canon
## (Canon in D)

Johann Pachelbel
Transcribed by Celeste Avery

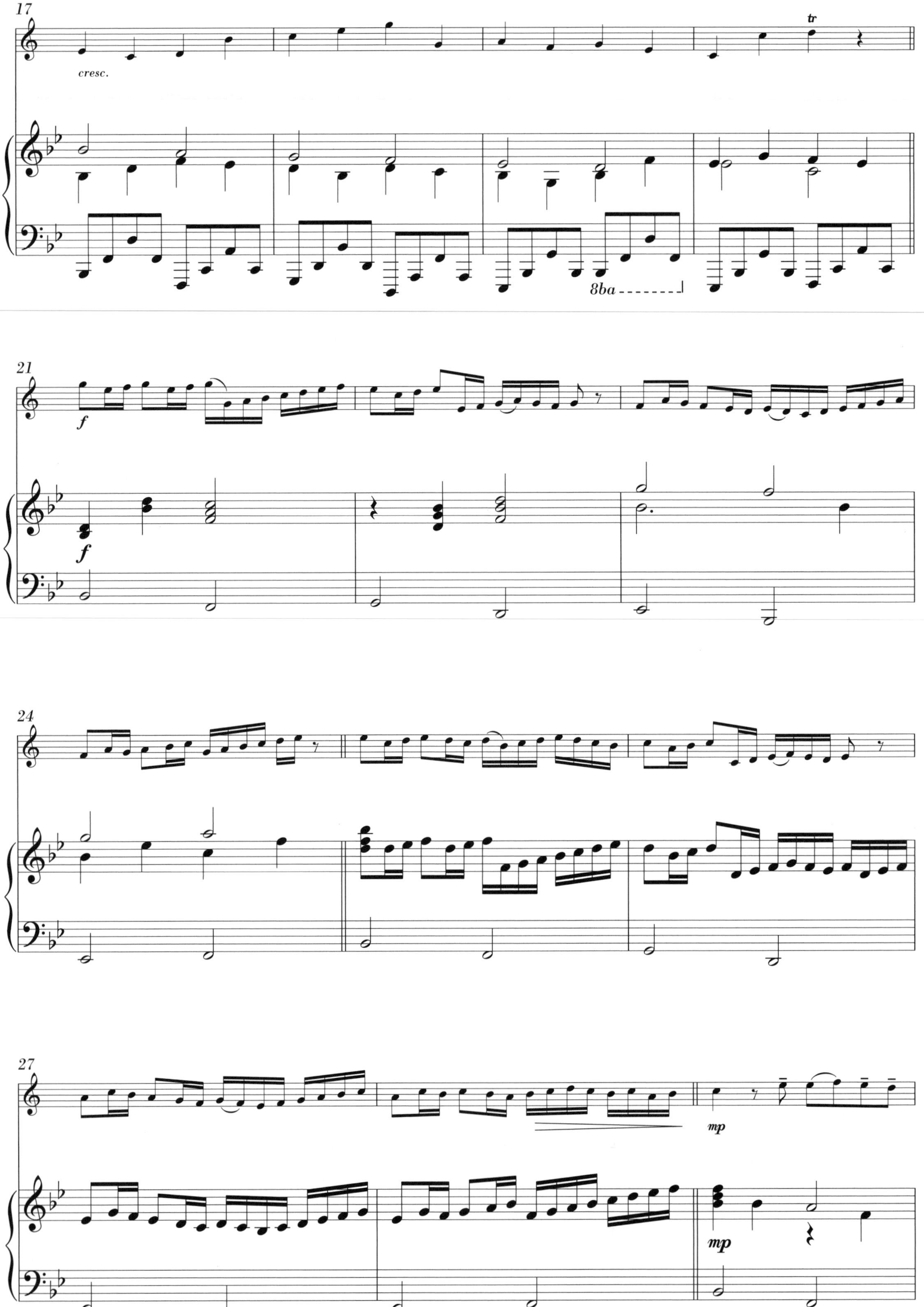
17
cresc.
tr
8ba
21
f
f
24
27
mp
mp

# Trumpet Tune

Henry Purcell
Transcribed by Christopher Ruck

# Gymnopédie No. 1

from *Trois Gymnopédies*

Erik Satie
Transcribed by Celeste Avery

For a shorter performance, the piece may begin at measure 40.

# Ave Maria

Franz Schubert
Transcribed by Celeste Avery

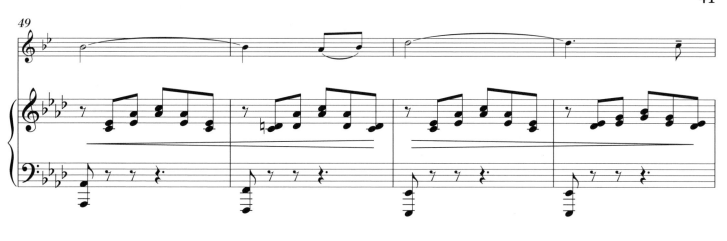

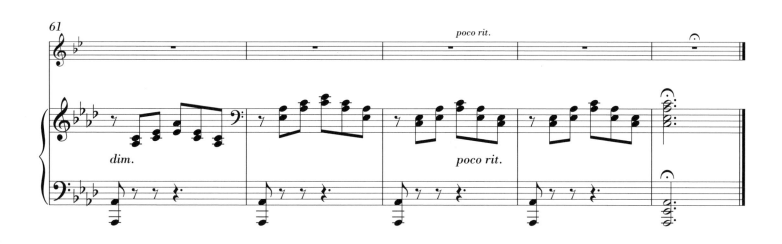

# Bist du bei mir
## (You Are with Me)

Gottfried Heinrich Stölzel
Transcribed by Celeste Avery

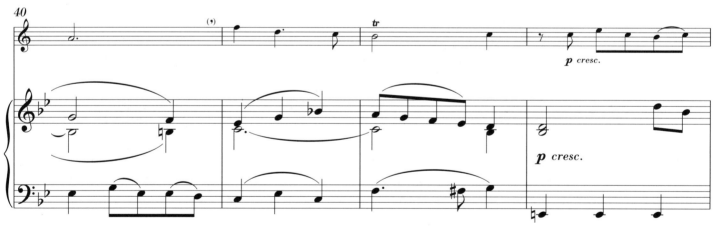